# Korean Conversations - Fun Korean Language Practice

# Learn Korean Fast Book I

Allen Williams PhD

Sulseob Jo PhD

PUBLISHED BY:
PowerMeUp Publishing
Copyright © 2012-2019
LearnKoreanFast.com

ISBN 9784907477042

All rights reserved.

No part of this publication may be copied, reproduced in any format, by any means, electronic or otherwise, without prior consent from the copyright owner and publisher of this book.

The conversations here are all a work of fiction. All characters, names, places and events are the product of the author's imagination or used fictitiously.

_____

# Table of Contents

Introduction

# Introduction

Skip this at your own risk!

All study is not bad. However, much of it is boring, and worse, a waste of time.

This book is neither of those things.

Why waste your time studying boring things or in a boring way? Just because it's the way most everyone is doing things?

This book is for any level of Korean language learner who can read and pronounce Hangul.

This is not a textbook in the usual sense. It is really more of a practice and example book. There are no "lessons" lain out for you.

Also, it's very unlikely you will ever have any of these conversations word for word in your real life.

In fact, these translations may at times not be exactly what a Korean might say in this situation, but it will be close. The reason is the conversations and sentences were constructed to give the closest of literal translation possibilities. So, there are no idioms, expressions, or anologies here. There are just straightforward sentences. Yes, there may be many other ways to translate them. That's not the point.

That may seem an odd statement to make at this point, but if you consider how many possibilities there are for most conversations other than "How are you?" and "I'm fine, and you?" there really are very few practice conversations in any textbook you might actually have word for word. Why not have fun learning some structures of conversation, some interesting and useful phrases, and exploring the language on your own rather than just be taught to parrot some conversations you will never actually have anyway?

These are practice conversations for you to get exposure to the way normal, comfortable conversations occur, and while there are of course a number of ways to translate or say the same thing in any language, the examples chosen are done so in a way to narrow down those choices.

Each conversation is intended to be both practical and interesting to help you to more easily remember the vocabulary. You will also see several short phrases that are repeated throughout various conversations. This will also help you through repetition to learn those phrases more easily by seeing them in context.

Each conversation is between two people who presumably know each other fairly well. This is important to keep in mind for context and for the levels of politeness either used or implied.

In fact, the situation is more helpful in aiding understanding than knowing the vocabulary, so invest a little time into understanding the context of each conversation you meet whether in this text of any other. It will help you to understand better and more quickly.

You will not find a lot of notes or explanations for several reasons. The main reasons being that by looking at the conversations and the translations you should be able to figure out on your own which parts go together, and the more of this connecting and figuring out you do on your own the easier it will be for you both to acquire the language and to remember it.

This also allows you to work at this at many different levels and at the levels that suit or interest you. For example, you might see some parts as simply being useful vocabulary or expressions, while someone else might notice that the sentence structure can be used for other instances by doing simple replacing of either the noun or the verb stem. You might also find that going over the conversations and memorizing them is great for you when you are a beginner, but as you progress, revisiting the conversations and digging deeper into the sentence structures can help you to expand your ability to communicate even more.

The font is intentionally a little large in order to help you to read the hangul characters a little more easily. Until you are really accustomed to the shapes of Korean words, it takes a little extra time to read some of the words, even when they are typed. Larger fonts help you to "look, then say" at a faster, more comfortable pace.

Some things to keep in mind as you go through this book:

- Korean language seldom uses the subject in sentences where it is understood. This is true for people or objects. That means there are very few instances where pronouns or "you" are used. "Are you okay?" in Korean roughly translates to "Okay?" more often than not.
- Yes, there are other ways to say what is being said in these conversations. Each translation has been done in order to reduce the amount of time you need to understand what part of the Korean sentence matches its corresponding part in the translated sentences.
- These conversations were originally written and structured in a way to facilitate translation. They are still as natural as possible in both Korean and in translation. While you may not ever (sometimes hopefully never) have need for any of these conversations word for word, any phrase you see here is current, appropriate vocabulary.
- Verbs come last. Korean is a verb driven language. Mostly you will see Subject (implied or understood as well) - Object - Verb sentence structures.
- There are many levels of Korean.
    - 1. Polite levels used for speaking to those who are older than you or above your social station.
    - 2. Moderate levels used to talk to those who are among your peer group.
    - 3. Low level (sometimes called 'impolite' as classification, and is when used in the wrong settings) used for speaking to someone much lower than your status in age or social position, but also used to show familiarity. This book tries to stick to the middle ground here. No one should be greatly offended by any of the usages here although it is probably not advisable to use them for talking to the president of your college or company.

That said, let's look at several ways you can use and benefit from these conversations.

- You can just read them and practice them alone by reading them aloud or to yourself.
- You can practice them with a partner. The dialogs are divided to separate pages for this.
- You can practice them along with the recordings.
- You can expand the conversations.
- Take a look at the sentences and see if there are any pieces you can work out that may even contain new vocabulary.
- Look for phrases and fragments that you can use in various contexts and situations.
- Most of all – have fun!

## 1. Can I ask you a big favor?

Hyocheol: Hey, how's it going?

Younghwa: Oh, hey. I guess things are okay.

Hyocheol: Really? What's the problem?

Younghwa: Ummm… Can I ask you a big favor?

Hyocheol: Of course.

Younghwa: Well, I need 1,000,000 won…

Hyocheol: Wow! I see… Why do you need so much money?

Younghwa: My car broke down, and I have to pay for the repairs.

Hyocheol: That's too bad. When do you need the money?

Younghwa: Actually I need it today before 5:00.

Hyocheol: Ok. I'll be happy to help you.

Younghwa: That's great. I really appreciate it.

Hyocheol: No problem. When can you pay me back?

Younghwa: I can pay you back after the first of next week without a doubt.

Hyocheol: Then, can you go with me now to the ATM?

Younghwa: That sounds great. And, really, I appreciate this.

Hyocheol: Oh, don't mention it. That's what friends are for. Let's go!

Younghwa: Yes, let's go.

1. 부탁 하나해도 돼?


효철 : 이 봐, 요즘 어때?

영화 : 음, 잘 지내고 있지? 그럭저럭 잘 지내고 있어.

효철 : 그래? 무슨 일 있나 보네?

영화 : 어 ... 부탁 하나해도 돼?

효철 : 그럼.

영화 : 어, 돈이 백만원 필요해 ...

효철 : 어! 그래 ... 왜 그렇게 많은 돈이 필요한데?

영화 : 타고 다니는 자동차가 고장이 나서, 수리비를 지불해야 해.

효철 : 그랬구나. 언제까지 필요해?

영화 : 실은, 오늘 오후 5 시가 기한이야.

효철 : 알겠어. 도와 주기로 하지.

영화 : 아, 잘 됐다. 참 고맙다.

효철 : 아니 뭘. 그런데 언제 갚을 거지?

영화 : 다음 주 초까지는 반드시 갚을 수 있어.

효철 : 그래, 그럼 나하고 지금 바로 ATM 가자?

영화 : 감사, 감사. 정말 고마워.

효철 : 뭘 이까짓 걸 가지고. 친구 사이에... 가자!

영화 : 그래, 가자.

1. 부탁 하나해도 돼?


효철 : 이 봐, 요즘 어때?

영화 : _____

효철 : 그래? 무슨 일 있나 보네?

영화 : _____

효철 : 그럼.

영화 : _____

효철 : 어! 그래 ... 왜 그렇게 많은 돈이 필요한데?

영화 : _____

효철 : 그랬구나. 언제까지 필요해?

영화 : _____

효철 : 알겠어. 도와 주기로 하지.

영화 : _____

효철 : 아니 뭘. 그런데 언제 갚을 거지?

영화 : _____

효철 : 그래, 그럼 나하고 지금 바로 ATM 가자?

영화 : _____

효철 : 뭘 이까짓 걸 가지고. 친구 사이에... 가자!

영화 : _____

1. 부탁 하나해도 돼?


효철 : _____

영화 : 음, 잘 지내고 있지? 그럭저럭 잘 지내고 있어.

효철 : _____

영화 : 어 ... 부탁 하나해도 돼?

효철 : _____

영화 : 어, 돈이 백만원 필요해 ...

효철 : _____

영화 : 타고 다니는 자동차가 고장이 나서, 수리비를 지불해야 해.

효철 : _____

영화 : 실은, 오늘 오후 5 시가 기한이야.

효철 : _____

영화 : 아, 잘 됐다. 참 고맙다.

효철 : _____

영화 : 다음 주 초까지는 반드시 갚을 수 있어.

효철 : _____

영화 : 감사, 감사. 정말 고마워.

효철 : _____

영화 : 그래, 가자.

**MY NOTES:**

## 2. That new Italian restaurant

Hyocheol: How's it going?

Younghwa: Great! How about you?

Hyocheol: I'm good, too.

Younghwa: Guess what I did last night?

Hyocheol: I know it wasn't study…

Younghwa: Come on.

Hyocheol: umm, laundry?

Younghwa: Stop joking around!

Hyocheol: Okay, I give up. What?

Younghwa: I went to that new Italian restaurant downtown.

Hyocheol: What? You know I've been dying to go there!

Younghwa: Oh? Really? I had no idea…

Hyocheol: Now you should stop joking around!

Younghwa: Ok. Ok. Don't get so excited!

Hyocheol: <sigh> So, tell me how was it?

Younghwa: Terrible! Really!

Hyocheol: I don't believe you.

Younghwa: Actually I didn't go, but I made a reservation for this evening.

Hyocheol: Oh?

Younghwa: So… if you still want to go…

Hyocheol: Oh, yeah! What time?

Younghwa: 7:20.

Hyocheol: Perfect!

Younghwa: I'll meet you there by 7:10, okay?

Hyocheol: Ok! I can't wait! Thanks!

Younghwa: See you there!

## 2. 새로 생긴 이탈리안 레스토랑

효철 : 잘 지내고 있어?

영화 : 잘 지내고 있지! 넌?

효철 : 나도 물론 잘 지내지.

영화 : 나 어제 저녁에 일 벌렸어.

효철 : 공부 열심히 했다는 소리는 아닐테고 ...

영화 : 무슨 소릴...

효철 : 음, 그럼 빨래 했어?

영화 : 농담 말고!

효철 : 아니, 진짜 모르겠어. 무슨 일 벌렸는데?

영화 : 시내에 새로 생긴 그 이탈리안 레스토랑에 갔었어.

효철 : 뭐라고? 내가 거기 얼마나 가고 싶어하는지 알면서...

영화 : 아? 그래? 난 정말 몰랐네 ...

효철 : 그만 놀려!

영화 : 알았어, 알았다고. 너무 화내지 마!

효철 : <한숨 쉬며> 그래, 거기 분위기 어떻디?

영화 : 너무 안 좋았어! 정말이지 실망!

효철 : 진짜야?

영화 : 실은 갔다는 건 거짓말, 근데 오늘 저녁에 간다고 예약 했음.

효철 : 으응?

영화 : 그래 ... 아직도 가고 싶은 마음이 있으신지 ...

효철 : 와우, 물론이지! 몇 시?

영화 : 7시 20 분.

효철 : 완전 좋아!

영화 : 7시 10분에 거기서 만나, 됐지?

효철 : 그럼! 빨리 가고 싶다! 고마우이!

영화 : 거기서 보자!

## 2. 새로 생긴 이탈리안 레스토랑

효철 : 잘 지내고 있어?

영화 : _____

효철 : 나도 물론 잘 지내지.

영화 : _____

효철 : 공부 열심히 했다는 소리는 아닐테고 ...

영화 : _____

효철 : 음, 그럼 빨래 했어?

영화 : _____

효철 : 아니, 진짜 모르겠어. 무슨 일 벌렸는데?

영화 : _____

효철 : 뭐라고? 내가 거기 얼마나 가고 싶어하는지 알면서...

영화 : _____

효철 : 그만 놀려!

영화 : _____

효철 : <한숨 쉬며> 그래, 거기 분위기 어떻디?

영화 : _____

효철 : 진짜야?

영화 : _____

효철 : 으응?

영화 : _____

효철 : 와우, 물론이지! 몇 시?

영화 : _____

효철 : 완전 좋아!

영화 : _____

효철 : 그럼! 빨리 가고 싶다! 고마우이!

영화 : _____

## 2. 새로 생긴 이탈리안 레스토랑

효철 : _____

영화 : 잘 지내고 있지! 넌?

효철 : _____

영화 : 나 어제 저녁에 일 벌렸어.

효철 : _____

영화 : 무슨 소릴...

효철 : _____

영화 : 농담 말고!

효철 : _____

영화 : 시내에 새로 생긴 그 이탈리안 레스토랑에 갔었어.

효철 : _____

영화 : 아? 그래? 난 정말 몰랐네 ...

효철 : _____

영화 : 알았어, 알았다고. 너무 화내지 마!

효철 : _____

영화 : 너무 안 좋았어! 정말이지 실망!

효철 : _____

영화 : 실은 갔다는 건 거짓말, 근데 오늘 저녁에 간다고 예약 했음.

효철 : _____

영화 : 그래 ... 아직도 가고 싶은 마음이 있으신지 ...

효철 : _____

영화 : 7시 20 분.

효철 : _____

영화 : 7시 10분에 거기서 만나, 됐지?

효철 : _____

영화 : 거기서 보자!

**MY NOTES:**

3. There's a rhinoceros in your car!

Hyocheol: There you are!

Younghwa: What?

Hyocheol: I was looking for you!

Younghwa: Why? What's up?

Hyocheol: I just saw the strangest thing.

Younghwa: Really? What does that have to do with me?

Hyocheol: Well, it was in your car.

Younghwa: My car?

Hyocheol: Yes.

Younghwa: What is it? What's wrong?

Hyocheol: I saw your car by chance, and there was a rhinoceros in it!

Younghwa: What are you talking about?

Hyocheol: I saw a rhinoceros in your car!

Younghwa: Are you sure you are okay? Do you have a fever?

Hyocheol: No fever! I'm fine! But not your car…

Younghwa: I'm sure my car is fine.

Hyocheol: Even with a rhinoceros in it?

Younghwa: You know my car is too small for a rhinoceros to fit inside it.

Hyocheol: But, I saw it. Really!

Younghwa: Where?

Hyocheol: In the front parking lot. It was right beside the front gate.

Younghwa: That's great.

Hyocheol: What?

Younghwa: It's no problem then. My car is in the back parking lot.

Hyocheol: That is a relief.

Younghwa: So, let's go have a cup of coffee.

Hyocheol: Sounds good to me.

## 3. 네 차 안에 코뿔소가 타고 있어!

효철 : 여기 있었네!

영화 : 무슨 일?

효철 : 너 찾고 있었어!

영화 : 왜? 무슨 일이냐고?

효철 : 좀전에 정말 괴상한 일을 목격했거든.

영화 : 정말? 나하고 상관 있는 일이야?

효철 : 그럼, 네 차 안에서 일어난 일인 걸.

영화 : 내 차 안에서 일어난 일?

효철 : 그래.

영화 : 무슨 일이야? 뭐가 괴상하다는 거지?

효철 : 내가 우연히 네 차를 보게 되었는데, 그 안에 코뿔소가 타고 있더라고!

영화 : 무슨 말을 하는 거야?

효철 : 네 차 안에 코뿔소가 타고 있더라니까...

영화 : 무슨 소리야? 열 있는 건 아니지?

효철 : 열이라니! 난 멀쩡해! 그래도 네 차는 멀쩡하지 못하지 .

영화 : 내 차야말로 멀쩡할 걸.

효철 : 차 안에 코뿔소가 있어도 문제 없다는 거지?

영화 : 야, 내 차 안에 코뿔소가 들어 갈 리가 만무하지.

효철 : 하지만, 난 봤어. 정말이야!

영화 : 어디?

효철 : 앞쪽 주차장. 바로 정문 옆에 있는 주차장.

영화 : 무슨 말인지 알 거 같네.

효철 : 무슨 대답이 그래?

영화 : 그 차는 내 차가 아니라고. 내 차는 뒤쪽 주차장에 세웠거든.

효철 : 휴, 이제야 안심이다.

영화 : 그럼 우리 커피나 한 잔 마시러 가.

효철 : 좋지.

3. 네 차 안에 코뿔소가 타고 있어!

효철 : 여기 있었네!

영화 : _____

효철 : 너 찾고 있었어!

영화 : _____

효철 : 좀전에 정말 괴상한 일을 목격했거든.

영화 : _____

효철 : 그럼, 네 차 안에서 일어난 일인 걸.

영화 : _____

효철 : 그래.

영화 : _____

효철 : 내가 우연히 네 차를 보게 되었는데, 그 안에 코뿔소가 타고 있더라고!

영화 : _____

효철 : 네 차 안에 코뿔소가 타고 있더라니까...

영화 : _____

효철 : 열이라니! 난 멀쩡해! 그래도 네 차는 멀쩡하지 못하지 .

영화 : _____.

효철 : 차 안에 코뿔소가 있어도 문제 없다는 거지?

영화 : _____

효철 : 하지만, 난 봤어. 정말이야!

영화 : _____

효철 : 앞쪽 주차장. 바로 정문 옆에 있는 주차장.

영화 : _____

효철 : 무슨 대답이 그래?

영화 : _____

효철 : 휴, 이제야 안심이다.

영화 : _____

효철 : 좋지.

## 3. 네 차 안에 코뿔소가 타고 있어!

효철 : _____

영화 : 무슨 일?

효철 : _____

영화 : 왜? 무슨 일이냐고?

효철 : _____

영화 : 정말? 나하고 상관 있는 일이야?

효철 : _____

영화 : 내 차 안에서 일어난 일?

효철 : _____

영화 : 무슨 일이야? 뭐가 괴상하다는 거지?

효철 : _____

영화 : 무슨 말을 하는 거야?

효철 : _____

영화 : 무슨 소리야? 열 있는 건 아니지?

효철 : _____

영화 : 내 차야말로 멀쩡할 걸.

효철 : _____

영화 : 야, 내 차 안에 코뿔소가 들어 갈 리가 만무하지.

효철 : _____

영화 : 어디?

효철 : _____

영화 : 무슨 말인지 알 거 같네.

효철 : _____

영화 : 그 차는 내 차가 아니라고. 내 차는 뒤쪽 주차장에 세웠거든.

효철 : _____

영화 : 그럼 우리 커피나 한 잔 마시러 가.

효철 : _____

**MY NOTES:**

## 4. At the tailor

Shop Owner: Come in!

Damin : Good afternoon.

Shop Owner: How can I help you?

Damin : I need to have a suit made.

Shop Owner: Sure. Let's get some measurements.

Damin : Oh, it's not for me. It's a gift.

Shop Owner: I see. Do you have the measurements?

Damin : Right here on this paper.

Shop Owner: Let me see. (Looks at the paper)

Damin : Is there a problem?

Shop Owner: It's very small.

Damin : Ah… yes, I know. Is that a problem?

Shop Owner: Maybe it's okay. Are these measurements correct?

Damin : Yes. Why do you ask?

Shop Owner: These sleeves seem a little long for such a small waist.

Damin : His arms are a little long.

Shop Owner: Okay. The legs seem a little short, too.

Damin : He's a little sensitive about that, but yes, it is correct.

Shop Owner: hmmm… Okay, but there's still something I'm not sure about.

Damin : What's that?

Shop Owner: Well, here it looks like you want a hole in the back of the pants.

Damin : Yes, that's right. It's for his tail?

Shop Owner: Tail?

Damin : Oh! This gift is for my monkey!

Shop Owner: Ahhh, now I see.

Damin : So you can do it?

Shop Owner: Sure. Let's pick out some material.

Damin : Yes, let's!

## 4. 양복점에서

상점 주인 : 어서 오세요!

다　　민 : 안녕하세요.

상점 주인 : 뭘 하시려고요?

다　　민 : 양복을 한 벌 맞출까 합니다.

상점 주인 : 네, 먼저 치수를 재어 볼까요.

다　　민 : 어, 제 게 아니고요. 선물할 겁니다.

상점 주인 : 그렇군요. 그럼 치수를 재어 오셨겠습니다.

다　　민 : 여기 이 종이에 적혀 있습니다.

상점 주인 : 어디 보십시다. (종이를 확인하고)

다　　민 : 무슨 문제가 있나요?

상점 주인 : 대단한 문제는 아닙니다.

다　　민 : 네, 그렇죠. 그게 문제가 되기는 하나요?

상점 주인 : 아마 괜찮을 겁니다. 여기 적힌 치수가 바로 맞기는 합니까?

다　　민 : 맞아요. 왜 그렇게 묻는 거죠?

상점 주인 : 이렇게 가는 허리를 가진 사람으로서는 소매 길이가 좀 길다 싶어서요.

다　　민 : 팔이 좀 긴 편입니다.

상점 주인 : 그래요. 다리는 좀 짧은 것 같은데요.

다　　민 : 본인도 그에 대해서는 좀 예민한 편이에요. 그런데, 말씀하시는대로 다리가 좀 짧아요.

상점 주인 : 흠 ... 그렇군요. 그런데 아직 이해가 안 가는 부분이 있어서.....

다　　민 : 그게 뭐죠?

상점 주인 : 바지 뒤 편에 구멍을 내어 달라고 하시는 것 같은데 이건 무슨 뜻입니까?.

다　　민 : 네, 말씀하신 그대로입니다. 그곳으로 꼬리를 내려고요.

상점 주인 : 꼬리요?

다　　민 : 네! 이건 내가 기르는 원숭이에게 선물할 양복입니다!

상점 주인 : 아~, 이제 캐취되었습니다.

다　　민 : 맞춰 줄 수 있겠습니까?

상점 주인 : 그럼요 맞춰 드리겠습니다. 이제 옷감을 골라 보시겠습니까.

다　　민 : 네, 옷감 고르기요!

## 4. 양복점에서

상점 주인 : 어서 오세요!

다　　민 : _____

상점 주인 : 뭘 하시려고요?

다　　민 : _____

상점 주인 : 네, 먼저 치수를 재어 볼까요.

다　　민 : _____

상점 주인 : 그렇군요. 그럼 치수를 재어 오셨겠습니다.

다　　민 : _____

상점 주인 : 어디 보십시다. (종이를 확인하고)

다　　민 : _____

상점 주인 : 대단한 문제는 아닙니다.

다　　민 : _____

상점 주인 : 아마 괜찮을 겁니다. 여기 적힌 치수가 바로 맞기는 합니까?

다　　민 : _____

상점 주인 : 이렇게 가는 허리를 가진 사람으로서는 소매 길이가 좀 길다 싶어서요.

다　　민 : _____

상점 주인 : 그래요. 다리는 좀 짧은 것 같은데요.

다　　민 : _____

상점 주인 : 흠 ... 그렇군요. 그런데 아직 이해가 안 가는 부분이 있어서.....

다　　민 : _____

상점 주인 : 바지 뒤 편에 구멍을 내어 달라고 하시는 것 같은데 이건 무슨 뜻입니까?.

다　　민 : _____

상점 주인 : 꼬리요?

다　　민 : _____

상점 주인 : 아~, 이제 캐취되었습니다.

다　　민 : _____

상점 주인 : 그럼요 맞춰 드리겠습니다. 이제 옷감을 골라 보시겠습니까.

다　　민 : _____

## 4. 양복점에서

상점 주인 : _____

다　　민 : 안녕하세요.

상점 주인 : _____

다　　민 : 양복을 한 벌 맞출까 합니다.

상점 주인 : _____.

다　　민 : 어, 제 게 아니고요. 선물할 겁니다.

상점 주인 : _____

다　　민 : 여기 이 종이에 적혀 있습니다.

상점 주인 : _____

다　　민 : 무슨 문제가 있나요?

상점 주인 : _____

다　　민 : 네, 그렇죠. 그게 문제가 되기는 하나요?

상점 주인 : _____

다　　민 : 맞아요. 왜 그렇게 묻는 거죠?

상점 주인 : _____

다　　민 : 팔이 좀 긴 편입니다.

상점 주인 : _____

다　　민 : 본인도 그에 대해서는 좀 예민한 편이에요. 그런데, 말씀하시는대로 다리가 좀 짧아요.

상점 주인 : _____

다　　민 : 그게 뭐죠?

상점 주인 : _____.

다　　민 : 네, 말씀하신 그대로입니다. 그곳으로 꼬리를 내려고요.

상점 주인 : _____

다　　민 : 네! 이건 내가 기르는 원숭이에게 선물할 양복입니다!

상점 주인 : _____

다　　민 : 맞춰 줄 수 있겠습니까?

상점 주인 : _____

다　　민 : 네, 옷감 고르기요!

**MY NOTES:**

5. On the way to the library

(Two friends passing each other on the sidewalk)

Hyocheol: Where are you going?

Younghwa: I'm on my way to the library.

Hyocheol: The library?

Younghwa: Yes, the library. Does it seem strange?

Hyocheol: Well, maybe. Do you often go to the library?

Younghwa: Actually in the summer time I often go there.

Hyocheol: Really? I had no idea you liked reading so much.

Younghwa: Oh, I enjoy reading a lot.

Hyocheol: What kinds of books do you read?

Younghwa: I read many different kinds. For example sometimes I read biographies, mysteries, and books on history.

Hyocheol: I see. That's very interesting. What area of history do you like most?

Younghwa: ummm… recent history…

Hyocheol: Recent? How recent?

Younghwa: This week.

Hyocheol: What?

Younghwa: Actually I'm reading a lot of celebrity magazines.

Hyocheol: Celebrity magazines?

Younghwa: Sure. They have biographies, mysteries, and what's going on these days!

Hyocheol: Arrrgghhh! I can't believe you sometimes.

Younghwa: And, I'm saving money on my electricity bill.

Hyocheol: How's that?

Younghwa: The library has free air conditioning!

Hyocheol: Of course you enjoy that!

Younghwa: Come with me! They also have free movies you can watch.

Hyocheol: Free movies?

Younghwa: Come on. Let's go.

5. 도서관에 가는 길에서

(두 친구가 인도에서 서로 지나치면서)

효철 : 어디 가는 길이야?

영화 : 도서관.

효철 : 도서관에?

영화 : 응, 도서관에. 이상해 보여?

효철 : 글쎄, 뭔가 좀... 도서관에는 자주 가?

영화 : 여름에는 자주 가지.

효철 : 그래? 네가 그렇게나 책읽기를 좋아한다고는 생각 안해 봤는 걸.

영화 : 으응, 내가 얼마나 책 읽기를 좋아하는데.

효철 : 어떤 책 좋아해?

영화 : 여러 가지. 예를 들면, 때로는 위인전, 때로는 미스테리, 때로는 역사 책을 읽기도 하고.

효철 : 응. 정말 멋지네. 주로 어떤 부분의 역사 책 읽어?

영화 : 흠 ... 최근에 생기는 일들 ...

효철 : 최근? 최근이라고 하면?

영화 : 이번 주.

효철 : 무슨 의미야?

영화 : 실은 유명인사들에 관한 잡지를 많이 읽고 있다는 거야.

효철 : 유명인사들에 관한 잡지?

영화 : 그럼. 그 안에는 위인들 이야기, 미스테리 이야기들 뿐만아니라, 최근에 어떤 일들이
일어나고 있는지도 함께 적혀 있어!

효철 : 어이쿠! 하여튼 넌 못말려.

영화 : 그리고, 우리 집 전기세도 절약하고 있지.

효철 : 그건 또 무슨 말?

영화 : 도서관에 가면 무료 에어컨 설비도 쓸 수 있거든!

효철 : 좋기도 하겠다!

영화 : 같이 가! 거기 가면 무료로 영화도 볼 수 있는 걸.

효철 : 무료 영화?

영화 : 가자. 같이 가 보자니까.

## 5. 도서관에가는 길에서

(두 친구가 인도에서 서로 지나치면서)

효철 : 어디 가는 길이야?

영화 : _____

효철 : 도서관에?

영화 : _____

효철 : 글쎄, 뭔가 좀... 도서관에는 자주 가?

영화 : _____

효철 : 그래? 네가 그렇게나 책읽기를 좋아한다고는 생각 안해 봤는 걸.

영화 : _____

효철 : 어떤 책 좋아해?

영화 : _____

효철 : 응. 정말 멋지네. 주로 어떤 부분의 역사 책 읽어?

영화 : _____

효철 : 최근? 최근이라고 하면?

영화 : _____

효철 : 무슨 의미야?

영화 : _____

효철 : 유명인사들에 관한 잡지?

영화 : _____

효철 : 어이쿠! 하여튼 넌 못말려.

영화 : _____

효철 : 그건 또 무슨 말?

영화 : _____

효철 : 좋기도 하겠다!

영화 : _____

효철 : 무료 영화?

영화 : _____

5. 도서관에가는 길에서
(두 친구가 인도에서 서로 지나치면서)

효철 : _____

영화 : 도서관.

효철 : _____

영화 : 응, 도서관에. 이상해 보여?

효철 : _____

영화 : 여름에는 자주 가지.

효철 : _____

영화 : 으응, 내가 얼마나 책 읽기를 좋아하는데.

효철 : _____

영화 : 여러 가지. 예를 들면, 때로는 위인전, 때로는 미스테리, 때로는 역사 책을 읽기도 하고.

효철 : _____

영화 : 흠 ... 최근에 생기는 일들 ...

효철 : _____

영화 : 이번 주.

효철 : _____

영화 : 실은 유명인사들에 관한 잡지를 많이 읽고 있다는 거야.

효철 : _____

영화 : 그럼. 그 안에는 위인들 이야기, 미스테리 이야기들 뿐만아니라, 최근에 어떤 일들이
일어나고 있는지도 함께 적혀 있어!

효철 : _____

영화 : 그리고, 우리 집 전기세도 절약하고 있지.

효철 : _____

영화 : 도서관에 가면 무료 에어컨 설비도 쓸 수 있거든!

효철 : _____

영화 : 같이 가! 거기 가면 무료로 영화도 볼 수 있는 걸.

효철 : _____

영화 : 가자. 같이 가 보자니까.

**MY NOTES:**

6. Are you okay?

Younghwa: Hey! Are you okay?

Hyocheol  : The truth is I don't feel so well.

Younghwa: What's the matter?

Hyocheol  : I have a bit of stomach ache.

Younghwa: Oh, I heard there's a bug going around.

Hyocheol  : That might be it, but maybe it's not.

Younghwa: Why do you say that?

Hyocheol  : I started feeling bad just now.

Younghwa: Something happened?

Hyocheol  : I think maybe I ate some bad food.

Younghwa: What kind of bad food? Where?

Hyocheol  : Ice cream. At the place you work.

Younghwa: No! That can't be.

Hyocheol  : I'm pretty sure I'm right.

Younghwa: How can you be sure?

Hyocheol  : Well, I went there, I ate ice cream, I came here, and now I don't feel good.

Younghwa: What kind of ice cream did you eat?

Hyocheol  : Some new flavors called strawberry lime, lemon and raisin, and kiwi and melon.

Younghwa: Well, those flavors don't sound very delicious to me.

Hyocheol  : At first they tasted okay, but not later.

Younghwa: What? How much did you eat?

Hyocheol  : Just some small sample sized cups.

Younghwa: Don't lie. Just that?

Hyocheol  : It's true.

Younghwa: Okay, then how many samples did you eat?

Hyocheol  : Ummm, 72.

Younghwa: You are very silly. You deserve to be sick.

Hyocheol  : Will you give me a ride home?

Younghwa: Okay, come on.

Hyocheol  : Thanks. Let's not stop for ice cream though.

## 6. 어디 아파?

영화 : 야! 어디 아파?

효철 : 실은 컨디션이 별로 좋지 않아.

영화 : 무슨 일인데?

효철 : 배가 좀 아픈 것 같아.

영화 : 어, 장 바이러스가 유행이라던데.

효철 : 그런 것도 같고, 아닌 것도 같고.

영화 : 무슨 말이야?

효철 : 방금 배가 아프기 시작했어.

영화 : 뭣 땜에?

효철 : 뭐 좀 안 좋은 걸 먹은 것 같아.

영화 : 안 좋은 거라니? 어디서?

효철 : 아이스크림. 네가 일하고 있는 그 아이스크림 가게에서 먹었잖아.

영화 : 아냐! 그게 나쁠 리가 없어.

효철 : 진짜야, 거기서 먹은 아이스크림이 문제인 거 같아.

영화 : 뭘로 그걸 확신하는 거지?

효철 : 아니, 거기 가서 아이스크림을 먹었고, 여기 돌아왔는데 배가 아프기 시작했다는 거지.

영화 : 무슨 맛 아이스크림 먹었어?

효철 : 딸기 라임 맛, 레몬 건포도 맛, 그리고 키위 멜론 맛이라고 새로 나온 맛이라던데.

영화 : 그래? 맛있기만 한 것들인데?

효철 : 막 맛보기 시작했을 때는 맛있기만 했지. 그런데 나중에는 아니더라고.

영화 : 뭐라고? 얼마나 먹은 거야?

효철 : 그냥 그 조그마한 시식용 사이즈 컵들이지.

영화 : 바른대로 말해. 그 것 뿐만이 아니지?

효철 : 실은 좀 더 먹었어.

영화 : 그래, 시식용 컵 몇 개 먹었어?

효철 : 음, 72개.

영화 : 아주 바보 짓을 했네. 배가 아프고도 싸죠.

효철 : 집까지 좀 태워 줄래?

영화 : 그래, 어서 타.

효철 : 고마워 태워 줘서. 하지만 아이스크림 가게는 들러지 말기로 하자.

## 6. 어디 아파?

영화 : 야! 어디 아파?

효철 : _____

영화 : 무슨 일인데?

효철 : _____

영화 : 어, 장 바이러스가 유행이라던데.

효철 : _____

영화 : 무슨 말이야?

효철 : _____

영화 : 뭣 땜에?

효철 : _____

영화 : 안 좋은 거라니? 어디서?

효철 : _____

영화 : 아냐! 그게 나쁠 리가 없어.

효철 : _____

영화 : 뭘로 그걸 확신하는 거지?

효철 : _____

영화 : 무슨 맛 아이스크림 먹었어?

효철 : _____

영화 : 그래? 맛있기만 한 것들인데?

효철 : _____

영화 : 뭐라고? 얼마나 먹은 거야?

효철 : _____

영화 : 바른대로 말해. 그 것 뿐만이 아니지?

효철 : _____

영화 : 그래, 시식용 컵 몇 개 먹었어?

효철 : _____

영화 : 아주 바보 짓을 했네. 배가 아프고도 싸죠.

효철 : _____

영화 : 그래, 어서 타.

효철 : _____

## 6. 어디 아파?

영화 : _____

효철 : 실은 컨디션이 별로 좋지 않아.

영화 : _____

효철 : 배가 좀 아픈 것 같아.

영화 : _____

효철 : 그런 것도 같고, 아닌 것도 같고.

영화 : _____

효철 : 방금 배가 아프기 시작했어.

영화 : _____

효철 : 뭐 좀 안 좋은 걸 먹은 것 같아.

영화 : _____

효철 : 아이스크림. 네가 일하고 있는 그 아이스크림 가게에서 먹었잖아.

영화 : _____

효철 : 진짜야, 거기서 먹은 아이스크림이 문제인 거 같아.

영화 : _____

효철 : 아니, 거기 가서 아이스크림을 먹었고, 여기 돌아왔는데 배가 아프기 시작했다는 거지.

영화 : _____

효철 : 딸기 라임 맛, 레몬 건포도 맛, 그리고 키위 멜론 맛이라고 새로 나온 맛이라던데.

영화 : _____

효철 : 막 맛보기 시작했을 때는 맛있기만 했지. 그런데 나중에는 아니더라고.

영화 : _____

효철 : 그냥 그 조그마한 시식용 사이즈 컵들이지.

영화 : _____

효철 : 실은 좀 더 먹었어.

영화 : _____

효철 : 음, 72개.

영화 : _____.

효철 : 집까지 좀 태워 줄래?

영화 : _____

효철 : 고마워 태워 줘서. 하지만 아이스크림 가게는 들러지 말기로 하자.

**MY NOTES:**

7. Studying for a test

Damin : Did you finish studying for tomorrow's test?

Dahyeon: Yeah, a little while ago.

Damin : How do you think you will do?

Dahyeon: hmmm, Maybe a little better than last time.

Damin : Oh yeah. That last test was pretty hard.

Dahyeon: But I did okay on that test without studying, so I'm not too worried.

Damin : Oh? I studied for it and still didn't get a good grade.

Dahyeon: That's too bad.

Damin : Yeah, if I didn't study at all, I can understand getting a low score.

Dahyeon: Sometimes that happens. Sometimes what you study isn't even on the test.

Damin : That's right. But this time I think I will be okay.

Dahyeon: Why do you think that?

Damin : I asked the teacher which parts were on the test!

Dahyeon: Ah! Good idea!

Damin : Last time I got only 40 points. This time I'm sure I'll do better.

Dahyeon: I got 40 points last time, too. That's not so bad.

Damin : Not so bad? 40 out of 100 is not good!

Dahyeon: 100? I thought it was a 50 point test!

Damin : So, are you ready to go now?

Dahyeon: No, I think I may have some more studying to do.

## 7. 시험 공부

다민 : 내일 시험 공부 끝냈어?

다현 : 응, 조금 전에.

다민 : 어떻게 될 거 같아?

다현 : 음~, 아마 지난 번보다는 좀 나을 거야.

다민 : 그래, 지난 번 시험은 꽤 어려웠어, 그지.

다현 : 그 시험에서 난 공부 안 하고도 꽤 괜찮은 성적을 받았거든. 그래서 이번에도 별 걱정은 안 해.

다민 : 아 그래? 나는 공부하고도 좋은 성적을 못 받았는데.

다현 : 참 안타까운 일이다.

다민 : 그러게나, 전혀 공부를 안 하고 나쁜 점수를 받았다면 이해가 가기도 하지만...

다현 : 때로 그런 일이 생기지. 어떤 때는 우리가 공부한 부분만 빼놓고 시험 문제가 출제되기도 하잖아.

다민 : 그래 그래. 근데 이번 만은 내 성적이 괜찮을 것이라 믿어.

다현 : 왜 그런 생각을 하지?

다민 : 어떤 문제가 나올 건지 선생님한테 물어 봤거든!

다현 : 어! 잘 했네!

다민 : 지난 번 시험에는 40 점 받았는데, 이 번에는 좀 더 나은 점수를 받는다는 말.

다현 : 나도 지난 번 시험에서 40 점 받았는데. 그만하면 괜찮은 점수라 할 수 있지 않아.

다민 : 괜찮은 점수라고? 100 점 만점에 40 점이 괜찮은 점수라고!

다현 : 100 점 만점의 시험? 50 점 만점의 시험이 아니고.

다민 : 그래, 이제 공부 다 했으니까 우리 나가도 돼?

다현 : 아니, 난 공부 좀 더 해야 돼.

## 7.시험 공부

다민 : 내일 시험 공부 끝냈어?

다현 : _____

다민 : 어떻게 될 거 같아?

다현 : _____

다민 : 그래, 지난 번 시험은 꽤 어려웠어, 그지.

다현 : _____

다민 : 아 그래? 나는 공부하고도 좋은 성적을 못 받았는데.

다현 : _____

다민 : 그러게나, 전혀 공부를 안 하고 나쁜 점수를 받았다면 이해가 가기도 하지만...

다현 : _____.

다민 : 그래 그래. 근데 이번 만은 내 성적이 괜찮을 것이라 믿어.

다현 : _____

다민 : 어떤 문제가 나올 건지 선생님한테 물어 봤거든!

다현 : _____

다민 : 지난 번 시험에는 40 점 받았는데, 이 번에는 좀 더 나은 점수를 받는다는 말.

다현 : _____

다민 : 괜찮은 점수라고? 100 점 만점에 40 점이 괜찮은 점수라고!

다현 : _____

다민 : 그래, 이제 공부 다 했으니까 우리 나가도 돼?

다현 : _____

7.시험 공부

다민 : _____

다현 : 응, 조금 전에.

다민 : _____

다현 : 음~, 아마 지난 번보다는 좀 나을 거야.

다민 : _____

다현 : 그 시험에서 난 공부 안 하고도 꽤 괜찮은 성적을 받았거든. 그래서 이번에도 별 걱정은 안 해.

다민 : _____

다현 : 참 안타까운 일이다.

다민 : _____

다현 : 때로 그런 일이 생기지. 어떤 때는 우리가 공부한 부분만 빼놓고 시험 문제가 출제되기도 하잖아.

다민 : _____

다현 : 왜 그런 생각을 하지?

다민 : _____

다현 : 어! 잘 했네!

다민 : _____

다현 : 나도 지난 번 시험에서 40 점 받았는데. 그만하면 괜찮은 점수라 할 수 있지 않아.

다민 : _____

다현 : 100 점 만점의 시험? 50 점 만점의 시험이 아니고.

다민 : _____

다현 : 아니, 난 공부 좀 더 해야 돼.

# MY NOTES:

8. Visiting a friend for the first time

(door bell rings)

Damin : Oh, hi! Come on in!

Dahyeon: Thanks! This is for you.

Damin : What's this?

Dahyeon: It's a present.

Damin : A present? What kind of present?

Dahyeon: Just because I've never visited your apartment before.

Damin : I know that, but you really didn't need to do that.

Dahyeon: Of course I did. What are you talking about?

Damin : It's Korean custom, but we're not in Korea now.

Dahyeon: It doesn't matter to me, and I couldn't come over empty handed.

Damin : Well, I appreciate it.

Dahyeon: Don't mention it.

Damin : Come on in.

Dahyeon: Here you go.

Damin : Wow, this is very heavy.

Dahyeon: Yeah, it was the biggest box of laundry detergent they had.

Damin : Laundry detergent?

Dahyeon: Yeah, they didn't have gift boxes of soaps or juice at the convenience store here.

Damin : I guess it's not the custom here.

Dahyeon: I'll say. The clerk thought I was crazy when I asked for gift boxes of tissue!

Damin : I'm sure!

## 8. 처음 가는 친구 집 방문

(현관 문 벨소리)

다민 : 헤이, 안녕! 어서 들어와!

다현 : 반갑다! 이거 써.

다민 : 이게 뭐지?

다현 : 선물이야.

다민 : 선물? 선물은 무슨 선물?

다현 : 네 집 방문하는 건 처음이잖아 .

다민 : 그건 그렇지만 뭐 이런 걸 사오고 그래.

다현 : 그래도~. 이게 한국 문화잖아?

다민 : 우리가 지금 한국에 살고 있는 것도 아닌데...

다현 : 아니 그래도... 빈 손으로 오기는 그래서.

다민 : 그래 어쨌든 고맙다.

다현 : 천만에 말씀을요.

다민 : 어서 들어 와

다현 : 여기 사 온 거.

다민 : 어이쿠,  너무 무겁다.

다현 : 응, 세탁용 세제. 가게에서 제일 큰 걸로 샀거든.

다민 : 세탁용 세제?

다현 : 그래, 비누나 주스 같은 선물용 박스 포장이 이 동네 편의점에는 없던 걸.

다민 : 이 사람들의 생활 습관은 아니니까.

다현 : 박스 포장이 된 비누 있냐고 하니까 점원이 어디서 온 정신병자인가 하고 생각하는 눈치더라고.

다민 : 그러고도 남았을 거다.

## 8. 처음 가는 친구 집 방문

(현관 문 벨소리)

다민 : 헤이, 안녕! 어서 들어와!

다현 : _____

다민 : 이게 뭐지?

다현 : _____

다민 : 선물? 선물은 무슨 선물?

다현 : _____

다민 : 그건 그렇지만 뭐 이런 걸 사오고 그래.

다현 : _____

다민 : 우리가 지금 한국에 살고 있는 것도 아닌데...

다현 : _____

다민 : 그래 어쨌든 고맙다.

다현 : _____

다민 : 어서 들어 와

다현 : _____

다민 : 어이쿠, 너무 무겁다.

다현 : _____

다민 : 세탁용 세제?

다현 : _____

다민 : 이 사람들의 생활 습관은 아니니까.

다현 : _____

다민 : 그러고도 남았을 거다.

## 8. 처음 가는 친구 집 방문

(현관 문 벨소리)

다민 : _____

다현 : 반갑다! 이거 써.

다민 : _____

다현 : 선물이야.

다민 : _____

다현 : 네 집 방문하는 건 처음이잖아 .

다민 : _____

다현 : 그래도~. 이게 한국 문화잖아?

다민 : _____

다현 : 아니 그래도... 빈 손으로 오기는 그래서.

다민 : _____

다현 : 천만에 말씀을요.

다민 : _____

다현 : 여기 사 온 거.

다민 : _____

다현 : 응, 세탁용 세제. 가게에서 제일 큰 걸로 샀거든.

다민 : _____

다현 : 그래, 비누나 주스 같은 선물용 박스 포장이 이 동네 편의점에는 없던 걸.

다민 : _____

다현 : 박스 포장이 된 비누 있냐고 하니까 점원이 어디서 온 정신병자인가 하고 생각하는 눈치더라고.

다민 : _____

**MY NOTES:**

9. Can you help me?

Hyocheol : Can you help me for a moment?

Dahyeon  : Sure, what do you need?

Hyocheol: I have to take these boxes up to my apartment.

Dahyeon  : Okay.

Hyocheol : Thanks.

Dahyeon  : Wow, this is pretty heavy.

Hyocheol : I know!

Dahyeon  : What's in it?

Hyocheol : Books!

Dahyeon  : Oh, I see. How are we going up?

Hyocheol : We have to take the stairs.

Dahyeon  : Stairs? Where's the elevator?

Hyocheol: This building is only 4 stories, so there isn't one.

Dahyeon  : Oh. What floor are we goin to?

Hyocheol : The 4th floor.

Dahyeon  : Of course.

Hyocheol : I really appreciate your help.

Dahyeon  : How come you look so sweaty? Isn't this your first load coming up?

Hyocheol : Yes, that's right.

Dahyeon  : So?

Hyocheol: Well, actually, these are the boxes that were supposed to stay in the apartment.

Dahyeon  : You must be kidding!

Hyocheol : No, sorry. I carried all of these down by mistake!

Dahyeon  : Well, you should have to carry them back by yourself!

Hyocheol : But you're a very good friend, so please help me.

Dahyeon  : Okay, but you really do owe me a big favor after this.

## 9. 좀 도와 줄 수 있어?

효철 : 잠깐 나 좀 도와 줄래?

다현 : 물론이지, 뭔데?

효철 : 이 상자들을 우리 집으로 옮겨야 돼.

다현 : 알았어.

효철 : 고마워.

다현 : 와, 이거 꽤 무거운데.

효철 : 그래, 꽤 무겁지?

다현 : 뭐가 들어 있는데?

효철 : 책!

다현 : 아, 이해가 간다. 어떻게 옮길 건데?

효철 : 계단으로 올라가야 해.

다현 : 계단? 엘리베이터는 없어?

효철 : 우리 아파트는 4 층 밖에 안되는 건물이잖아. 엘리베이터는 없지.

다현 : 으응, 니네 집은 몇 층?

효철 : 4 (사)층.

다현 : 완전 일 되네.

효철 : 도와줘서 정말 고마워.

다현 : 왜 그렇게 땀 투성이지? 처음 나르는 짐 아냐?

효철 : 그러게나 말이다.

다현 : 그런데?

효철 : 으음, 실은 이 박스들은 그냥 집에 두었어야 할 상자들인데...

다현 : 뭐라고? 자알 하셨네!

효철 : 아니, 정말 멍청한 짓을 한거야. 이 상자들은 다 집에 남겨 둬야 할 상자들인 걸 그만.

다현 : 그럼 전부 네가 혼자서 갖다 날라야 겠네.

효철 : 어-, 우리는 좋은 친구 사이지, 제발 날 좀 도와 주시게.

다현 : 오케이, 도와주는 대신 한 턱 크게 쓰기다.

9. 좀 도와 줄 수 있어?

효철 : 잠깐 나 좀 도와 줄래?
다현 : _____
효철 : 이 상자들을 우리 집으로 옮겨야 돼.
다현 : _____
효철 : 고마워.
다현 : _____
효철 : 그래, 꽤 무겁지?
다현 : _____
효철 : 책!
다현 : _____
효철 : 계단으로 올라가야 해.
다현 : _____
효철 : 우리 아파트는 4 층 밖에 안되는 건물이잖아. 엘리베이터는 없지.
다현 : _____
효철 : 4 (사)층.
다현 : _____
효철 : 도와줘서 정말 고마워.
다현 : _____
효철 : 그러게나 말이다.
다현 : _____
효철 : 으음, 실은 이 박스들은 그냥 집에 두었어야 할 상자들인데...
다현 : _____
효철 : 아니, 정말 멍청한 짓을 한거야. 이 상자들은 다 집에 남겨 둬야 할 상자들인 걸 그만.
다현 : _____
효철 : 어-, 우리는 좋은 친구 사이지, 제발 날 좀 도와 주시게.
다현 : _____

9. 좀 도와 줄 수 있어?

효철 : _____

다현 : 물론이지, 뭔데?

효철 : _____

다현 : 알았어.

효철 : _____

다현 : 와, 이거 꽤 무거운데.

효철 : _____

다현 : 뭐가 들어 있는데?

효철 : _____

다현 : 아, 이해가 간다. 어떻게 옮길 건데?

효철 : _____

다현 : 계단? 엘리베이터는 없어?

효철 : _____

다현 : 으응, 니네 집은 몇 층?

효철 : _____

다현 : 완전 일 되네.

효철 : _____

다현 : 왜 그렇게 땀 투성이지? 처음 나르는 짐 아냐?

효철 : _____

다현 : 그런데?

효철 : _____

다현 : 뭐라고? 자알 하셨네!

효철 : _____

다현 : 그럼 전부 네가 혼자서 갖다 날라야 겠네.

효철 : _____

다현 : 오케이, 도와주는 대신 한 턱 크게 쓰기다.

**MY NOTES:**

## 10. Let's go sing!

Younghwa: What are you doing tonight?

Damin    : Nothing special. Why do you ask?

Younghwa: I thought we could go do karaoke.

Damin    : Okay, I haven't been for a long time.

Younghwa: Great. How about meeting me here at about 7, and we'll go together?

Damin    : Sounds good. By the way, who else is going?

Younghwa: Maybe 3 or 4 other people, but I'm not really sure.

Damin    : Oh, okay. Do I know them?

Younghwa: Yes, it's Hyocheol and Dahyeon and 2 of their friends.

Damin    : I see.

Younghwa: What? Is that a problem?

Damin    : No, no. It's okay.

Younghwa: It's just one time.

Damin    : I know. I know.

Younghwa: And it's just for fun.

Damin    : But Hyocheol is totally tone deaf!

Younghwa: Remember that going to karaoke is all about enjoying yourself. It's not about singing well.

Damin    : I know that, but it's hard to enjoy myself with both hands over my ears!

Younghwa: Come on! It's not that bad.

Damin    : Yes it is. You'll see!

Younghwa: Haha, okay. See you at 7:00.

Damin    : Okay, see you later.

## 10. 노래방 가자!

영화 : 오늘 밤 스케줄 있어?

다민 : 뭐 별일 없는데. 왜 묻는 거지?

영화 : 노래방이나 갈까 하고.

다민 : 좋아, 오랫 동안 못 갔네.

영화 : 좋았어. 그럼 여기서 7 시에 만나서 함께 가는 게 어때?

다민 : 그러자. 그런데 누가누가 가기로 했지?

영화 : 대 여섯 사람쯤. 하지만 아직 정확히는 모르겠어.

다민 : 어, 알았어. 내가 아는 사람들이긴 해?

영화 : 응, 효철이하고 다현이, 그리고 그 친구들 친구 둘.

다민 : 그렇구나.

영화 : 왜? 그게 문제가 돼?

다민 : 아니, 아냐. 괜찮아.

영화 : 딱 한 번만이다.

다민 : 알겠어, 알고 있다고.

영화 : 그리고 그냥 재미로 한 번.

다민 : 효철이는 완전 음치인 거 알지!

영화 : 노래방에 가는 건 그냥 즐기는 데 의미가 있지, 노래를 잘하고 못하고의 문제가 아니잖아.

다민 : 그래, 그러긴 해도 그 음치들 노래하는 거 들으면서 즐거워지기나 한대?

영화 : 야, 그만큼 나쁘지는 않지.

다민 : 나쁘고 말고. 금새 두손 들거야!

영화 : 하하, 알겠어. 7(일곱) 시에 보자.

다민 : 오케이, 그 때 봐.

10. 노래방 가자!

영화 : 오늘 밤 스케줄 있어?
다민 : _____

영화 : 노래방이나 갈까 하고.
다민 : _____

영화 : 좋았어. 그럼 여기서 7시에 만나서 함께 가는 게 어때?
다민 : _____

영화 : 대 여섯 사람쯤. 하지만 아직 정확히는 모르겠어.
다민 : _____

영화 : 응, 효철이하고 다현이, 그리고 그 친구들 친구 둘.
다민 : _____

영화 : 왜? 그게 문제가 돼?
다민 : _____

영화 : 딱 한 번만이다.
다민 : _____

영화 : 그리고 그냥 재미로 한 번.
다민 : _____

영화 : 노래방에 가는 건 그냥 즐기는 데 의미가 있지, 노래를 잘하고 못하고의 문제가 아니잖아.
다민 : _____

영화 : 야, 그만큼 나쁘지는 않지.
다민 : _____

영화 : 하하, 알겠어. 7(일곱) 시에 보자.
다민 : _____

10. 노래방 가자!

영화 : _____

다민 : 뭐 별일 없는데. 왜 묻는 거지?

영화 : _____

다민 : 좋아, 오랫 동안 못 갔네.

영화 : _____

다민 : 그러자. 그런데 누가누가 가기로 했지?

영화 : _____

다민 : 어, 알았어. 내가 아는 사람들이긴 해?

영화 : _____

다민 : 그렇구나.

영화 : _____

다민 : 아니, 아냐. 괜찮아.

영화 : _____

다민 : 알겠어, 알고 있다고.

영화 : _____

다민 : 효철이는 완전 음치인 거 알지!

영화 : _____

다민 : 그래, 그러긴 해도 그 음치들 노래하는 거 들으면서 즐거워지기나 한대?

영화 : _____

다민 : 나쁘고 말고. 금새 두손 들거야!

영화 : _____

다민 : 오케이, 그 때 봐.

**MY NOTES:**

## 11. How do you eat an elephant?

Damin : How was class today?

Dahyeon: Interesting, but the teacher asked me a strange question.

Damin : What was it about?

Dahyeon: It was about eating an elephant.

Damin : Really? That does sound a little strange.

Dahyeon: I thought so, too.

Damin : Well, what was the question?

Dahyeon: He asked, "Do you know the best way to eat an elephant?"

Damin : Ha! That's a classic question.

Dahyeon: Really? Even so. It's the first time I heard it.

Damin : So, did you know the answer?

Dahyeon: I didn't know, and even worse I couldn't understand the answer.

Damin : Why not?

Dahyeon: I understood the words but not the meaning.

Damin : I see. That's very frustrating.

Dahyeon: He said the answer was to eat it one bite at a time.

Damin : But he didn't explain it?

Dahyeon: Not really. He said to work it out.

Damin : It means that you have to tackle big tasks the same as small ones: one step at a time.

Dahyeon: Oh, I get it now.

Damin : Great. Do you know the best way to eat a cow?

Dahyeon: Yeah! Hamburgers! Let's go!

Damin : Let's take my car.

Dahyeon: Even better!

## 11. 어떻게 코끼리를 먹지?

다민 : 오늘 수업 어땠어?

다현 : 흥미로웠음. 그런데 선생님이 이상한 질문을 하셨어.

다민 : 어떤 질문?

다현 : 코끼리를 먹고 어쩌고....

다민 : 뭐라고? 그거 꽤 이상한 소리네.

다현 : 누가 아니래.

다민 : 음, 질문이 어땠는데?

다현 : "코끼리를 잘 먹을 수 있는 가장 좋은 방법" 에 대해서 말해 보라고 질문하셨어.

다민 : 으응 그거! 그건 아주 고전적인 질문이잖아.

다현 : 그래? 그래도 나는 처음 듣는 말이었는데.

다민 : 그래, 답은 알았어?

다현 : 몰랐지. 질문 내용조차 파악 못했는 걸.

다민 : 왜?

다현 : 아니, 말을 몰라서가 아니라 의미 접수가 안 됐지.

다민 : 그래. 아주 안타까운 일이지.

다현 : 선생님의 대답이 "그건 한 번에 한 입씩 먹는 거"랬어.

다민 : 왜 그런가에 대한 설명은 없었어?

다현 : 아니. 곰곰히 생각해서 알아 맞춰 보라시더라고.

다민 : 그건 아무리 큰 일이더라도 작은 일을 해 내는 거와 마찬가지로 한 번에 한 단계씩 밟아서 진행해야 한다는 거지.

다현 : 아, 이제 알았다.

다민 : 좋았어. 그럼 소를 잘 먹을 수 있는 가장 좋은 방법은?

다현 : 물론! 그건 햄버거 만들어서 먹는 거! 햄버거 먹으러 가자!

다민 : 내 차로 갈까.

다현 : 그거 좋지!

## 11. 어떻게 코끼리를 먹지?

다민 : 오늘 수업 어땠어?

다현 : _____

다민 : 어떤 질문?

다현 : _____

다민 : 뭐라고? 그거 꽤 이상한 소리네.

다현 : _____

다민 : 음, 질문이 어땠는데?

다현 : _____

다민 : 으응 그거! 그건 아주 고전적인 질문이잖아.

다현 : _____

다민 : 그래, 답은 알았어?

다현 : _____

다민 : 왜?

다현 : _____

다민 : 그래. 아주 안타까운 일이지.

다현 : _____

다민 : 왜 그런가에 대한 설명은 없었어?

다현 : _____

다민 : 그건 아무리 큰 일이더라도 작은 일을 해 내는 거와 마찬가지로 한 번에 한 단계씩 밟아서 진행해야 한다는 거지.

다현 : _____

다민 : 좋았어. 그럼 소를 잘 먹을 수 있는 가장 좋은 방법은?

다현 : _____

다민 : 내 차로 갈까.

다현 : _____

## 11. 어떻게 코끼리를 먹지?

다민 : _____

다현 : 흥미로웠음. 그런데 선생님이 이상한 질문을 하셨어.

다민 : _____

다현 : 코끼리를 먹고 어쩌고....

다민 : _____

다현 : 누가 아니래.

다민 : _____

다현 : "코끼리를 잘 먹을 수 있는 가장 좋은 방법" 에 대해서 말해 보라고 질문하셨어.

다민 : _____

다현 : 그래? 그래도 나는 처음 듣는 말이었는데.

다민 : _____

다현 : 몰랐지. 질문 내용조차 파악 못했는 걸.

다민 : _____

다현 : 아니, 말을 몰라서가 아니라 의미 접수가 안 됐지.

다민 : _____

다현 : 선생님의 대답이 "그건 한 번에 한 입씩 먹는 거"랬어.

다민 : _____

다현 : 아니. 곰곰히 생각해서 알아 맞춰 보라시더라고.

다민 : _____

다현 : 아, 이제 알았다.

다민 : _____

다현 : 물론! 그건 햄버거 만들어서 먹는 거! 햄버거 먹으러 가자!

다민 : _____

다현 : 그거 좋지!

**MY NOTES:**

12. What did you do for the weekend?

Hyocheol: Hey! How was your weekend?

Damin　　: Pretty good. How about you?

Hyocheol: It was okay.

Damin　　: That's good.

Hyocheol: So, what did you do?

Damin　　: Saturday morning I went downtown to shop for a birthday present for my father.

Hyocheol: Ah… what did you get for him?

Damin　　: I got him a book about trees.

Hyocheol: A book about trees?

Damin　　: Yes, he loves hiking and looking at the plants and things along the way.

Hyocheol: Then I'm sure he'll like that.

Damin　　: I hope so.

Hyocheol: What was next?

Damin　　: Then I went to my part-time job until late.

Hyocheol: What about Sunday?

Damin　　: I didn't do anything really special. I slept a little late, watched TV, and read some of the books I bought for my dad.

Hyocheol: What did you do after that?

Damin　　: hmmm… I met a classmate to study for today's test.

Hyocheol: Test? Today?

Damin　　: Sure. You forgot?

Hyocheol: I remember something now though.

Damin　　: What's that?

Hyocheol: I feel a little sick, so I have to go back home now. Bye.

Damin　　: Okay…

## 12. 주말에 뭐 했어?

효철 : 헤이! 주말 잘 보냈어?

다민 : 꽤 괜찮았지. 넌?

효철 : 그럭저럭.

다민 : 나쁘지는 않았네.

효철 : 그래, 뭐 했는데?

다민 : 토요일 아침에 시내에 갔어. 아버지 생신 선물 사려고.

효철 : 아 ... 뭘로 샀어?

다민 : 책 한 권 샀어. 나무에 관한 책.

효철 : 나무에 관한 책?

다민 : 응, 아버지는 하이킹하면서 길 가에 심겨진 풀과 나무들을 관찰하시는 걸 좋아하시거든.

효철 : 그렇다면 아버지께서 그 선물을 받으시고 좋아하시겠네.

다민 : 그럴 거야.

효철 : 그거뿐이야?

다민 : 그 다음에는 늦게까지 알바 했어.

효철 : 일요일은 뭐 했어?

다민 : 별 거 안 했어. 조금 늦게까지 자고 일어나서, TV 좀 보고, 그리고 아버지 생신 선물로 산 책도 좀 읽었어.

효철 : 그 다음에는 뭐 했냐구?

다민 : 흠 ... 오늘 시험을 위해서 친구 만나 공부했지.

효철 : 테스트라고? 오늘?

다민 : 그래. 오늘 시험 있는 거 몰라?

효철 : 이제 뭔가 생각이 나는 듯도 해.

다민 : 그게 뭔데?

효철 : 어, 컨디션이 좀 안 좋아. 나 지금 집에 가 봐야겠어. 바이바이.

다민 : 일만드는군 ...

12. 주말에 뭐 했어?

효철 : 헤이! 주말 잘 보냈어?

다민 : _____

효철 : 그럭저럭.

다민 : _____

효철 : 그래, 뭐 했는데?

다민 : _____

효철 : 아 … 뭘로 샀어?

다민 : _____

효철 : 나무에 관한 책?

다민 : _____

효철 : 그렇다면 아버지께서 그 선물을 받으시고 좋아하시겠네.

다민 : _____

효철 : 그거뿐이야?

다민 : _____

효철 : 일요일은 뭐 했어?

다민 : _____

효철 : 그 다음에는 뭐 했냐구?

다민 : _____

효철 : 테스트라고? 오늘?

다민 : _____

효철 : 이제 뭔가 생각이 나는 듯도 해.

다민 : _____

효철 : 어, 컨디션이 좀 안 좋아. 나 지금 집에 가 봐야겠어. 바이바이.

다민 : _____

12. 주말에 뭐 했어?

효철 : _____

다민 : 꽤 괜찮았지. 넌?

효철 : _____

다민 : 나쁘지는 않았네.

효철 : _____

다민 : 토요일 아침에 시내에 갔어. 아버지 생신 선물 사려고.

효철 : _____

다민 : 책 한 권 샀어. 나무에 관한 책.

효철 : _____

다민 : 응, 아버지는 하이킹하면서 길 가에 심겨진 풀과 나무들을 관찰하시는 걸 좋아하시거든.

효철 : _____

다민 : 그럴 거야.

효철 : _____

다민 : 그 다음에는 늦게까지 알바 했어.

효철 : _____

다민 : 별 거 안 했어. 조금 늦게까지 자고 일어나서, TV 좀 보고, 그리고 아버지 생신 선물로 산 책도 좀 읽었어.

효철 : _____

다민 : 흠 ... 오늘 시험을 위해서 친구 만나 공부했지.

효철 : _____

다민 : 그래. 오늘 시험 있는 거 몰라?

효철 : _____

다민 : 그게 뭔데?

효철 : _____

다민 : 일만드는군 ...

**MY NOTES:**

## 13. Big black dog!

Damin : Did you see that dog outside?

Hyocheol: What dog?

Damin : There was a big black dog outside when I came in.

Hyocheol: I didn't see anything.

Damin : How could you have missed seeing it?

Hyocheol: I came in early, so I guess it wasn't there then.

Damin : Well, it's huge!

Hyocheol: Where did you see it?

Damin : It was right beside the door.

Hyocheol: Was somebody with the dog?

Damin : I don't think so.

Hyocheol: Well, were other people bothered by it?

Damin : Some people were, but other people just walked right by it like it wasn't there.

Hyocheol: Well, that part is a little strange.

Damin : It thought so, too.

Hyocheol: Should we call the security office (building security? Police?)?

Damin : Maybe.

Hyocheol: Okay. Let's do that. Tell me again what you saw.

Damin : Okay. It was a big, black dog.

Hyocheol: How big?

Damin : hmmm… about as tall as you.

Hyocheol: What? Wow! Really? Just sitting there?

Damin : Standing.

Hyocheol: Just standing?

Damin : Well, it was handing out flyers about pet care.

Hyocheol: arrrggghhh!!! It was somebody in a dog suit?

Damin : Maybe. Here's one of the flyers.

Hyocheol: You're making me crazy!

## 13. 커다란 검둥이!

다민 : 밖에 있는 그 개 봤어?

효철 : 개라고?

다민 : 내가 들어 올 때 바깥에 커다란 검둥이가 한 마리 있었는데.

효철 : 아무 것도 없었어.

다민 : 어떻게 그걸 못 볼 수 있지?

효철 : 나 아까 들어 왔어. 그래서 그 때는 아직 거기 없었나 보지.

다민 : 흐음, 아주 컸는데!

효철 : 어디서 봤다는 거야?

다민 : 대문 바로 옆에.

효철 : 개하고 누가 같이 있었어?

다민 : 아무도 없었어.

효철 : 응, 다른 사람들이 무서워 했어?

다민 : 일부 사람들은 무서워 하더라고. 대부분의 사람들은 거기 아무 것도 없는 것처럼 그냥 스쳐 지나갔고.

효철 : 그래, 그 부분이 좀 이상하다.

다민 : 나도 그렇게 생각해.

효철 : 보안 사무실 (수위실? 경찰?)에 연락해야 할까?

다민 : 그럴까.

효철 : 그래. 연락하자. 다시 한 번 상황 설명을 좀 해 봐.

다민 : 응. 커다란 검둥이가 ...

효철 : 얼마나 커?

다민 : 음 ... 네 덩치만 해.

효철 : 뭐라고? 그렇게나 커! 정말? 그냥 거기 앉아 있었어?

다민 : 서 있었어.

효철 : 그냥 서 있었어?

다민 : 음, 반려 동물에 대한 전단지 나눠 주고 있었어.

효철 : 이런 이런! 그건 개 모습으로 분장한 사람이야?

다민 : 그런가. 이게 그 전단지야.

효철 : 사람 미치게 하는 군!

## 13. 커다란 검둥이!

다민 : 밖에 있는 그 개 봤어?

효철 : _____

다민 : 내가 들어 올 때 바깥에 커다란 검둥이가 한 마리 있었는데.

효철 : _____

다민 : 어떻게 그걸 못 볼 수 있지?

효철 : _____

다민 : 흐음, 아주 컸는데!

효철 : _____

다민 : 대문 바로 옆에.

효철 : _____

다민 : 아무도 없었어.

효철 : _____

다민 : 일부 사람들은 무서워 하더라고. 대부분의 사람들은 거기 아무 것도 없는 것처럼 그냥 스쳐 지나갔고.

효철 : _____

다민 : 나도 그렇게 생각해.

효철 : _____

다민 : 그럴까.

효철 : _____

다민 : 응. 커다란 검둥이가 ...

효철 : _____

다민 : 음 ... 네 덩치만 해.

효철 : _____

다민 : 서 있었어.

효철 : _____

다민 : 음, 반려 동물에 대한 전단지 나눠 주고 있었어.

효철 : _____

다민 : 그런가. 이게 그 전단지야.

효철 : _____

13. 커다란 검둥이!

다민 : _____

효철 : 개라고?

다민 : _____

효철 : 아무 것도 없었어.

다민 : _____

효철 : 나 아까 들어 왔어. 그래서 그 때는 아직 거기 없었나 보지.

다민 : _____

효철 : 어디서 봤다는 거야?

다민 : _____

효철 : 개하고 누가 같이 있었어?

다민 : _____

효철 : 응, 다른 사람들이 무서워 했어?

다민 : _____

효철 : 그래, 그 부분이 좀 이상하다.

다민 : _____

효철 : 보안 사무실 (수위실?  경찰?)에 연락해야 할까?

다민 : _____

효철 : 그래. 연락하자. 다시 한 번 상황 설명을 좀 해 봐.

다민 : _____

효철 : 얼마나 커?

다민 : _____

효철 : 뭐라고? 그렇게나 커! 정말? 그냥 거기 앉아 있었어?

다민 : _____

효철 : 그냥 서 있었어?

다민 : _____

효철 : 이런 이런! 그건 개 모습으로 분장한 사람이야?

다민 : _____

효철 : 사람 미치게 하는 군!

**MY NOTES:**

## 14. Drive your car

Jeonghwa: Hey, how's it going?

Dahyeon : Good. Thanks. How about you?

Jeonghwa: Good. Good.

Dahyeon : I was wondering if you were driving your car to school tomorrow.

Jeonghwa: I wasn't really planning to do that. Why?

Dahyeon : I see. Well, tomorrow there will be some construction outside our building.

Jeonghwa: So?

Dahyeon : Well, some people were asked to not leave their cars in the parking lot.

Jeonghwa: I see. Well, I didn't hear anything about that.

Dahyeon : That's odd. There were lots of notices.

Jeonghwa: But this is the first time I've heard about it.

Dahyeon : Anyway there will be a lot of dust and big trucks moving in and out.

Jeonghwa: Maybe my car will be okay.

Dahyeon : Are you sure you want to take a chance your car will get damaged?

Jeonghwa: I think it will be okay.

Dahyeon : Well, I wouldn't take any chance if it was my car.

Jeonghwa: Then, what about your car?

Dahyeon : Oh, my car is in the shop.

Jeonghwa: And the only reason you want me to take my car is to keep it safe?

Dahyeon : Of course!

Jeonghwa: If I drive my car, do you want me to give you a ride?

Dahyeon : Oh, that's a good idea! Thanks!

Jeonghwa: You're welcome.

## 14. 자동차로 가?

종하 : 헤이, 잘 지내고 있어?

다현 : 다 괜찮아. 고맙고. 넌 어때?

종하 : 좋아. 다 괜찮아.

다현 : 내일 학교 차 몰고 갈 거야?

종하 : 그런 생각 없었는데, 왜?

다현 : 응. 내일 아파트 근처에 공사가 있을 거거든.

종하 : 그런데?

다현 : 음, 주차장에 차 두지 말라는 얘기가 있었다 하더라고.

종하 : 그랬구나. 글쎄, 난 아무 소리도 못 들었는데.

다현 : 이상하네. 여기저기서 통지가 있었다는데.

종하 : 하지만 난 처음으로 듣는 말인 걸.

다현 : 어쨌든 큰 트럭이 왔다갔다 하면서 먼지가 많이 날 거야.

종하 : 내 차는 괜찮아.

다현 : 네 차량이 손상되는 일이 있어도 괜찮다는 뜻인가?

종하 : 문제 없을 거야.

다현 : 글쎄다. 나라면 절대로 위험은 감수하지 않을 텐데...

종하 : 그러면 네 차는 어떻게 할 건데?

다현 : 어, 내 차는 지금 수리 가게에 있어.

종하 : 그래, 학교에 차 몰고 가는지 어떤지를 묻는 이유가 달리 있었구만. 공사 중에 먼지 안 쓰게 하는 게 이유는 아닌 거 같은데?

다현 : 당근이지!

종하 : 내가 차 몰고 학교 가면 태워다 드릴까?

다현 : 아, 그거 참 좋은 생각이네! 고마우이!

종하 : 천만에 ...

14. 자동차로 가?

종하 : 헤이, 잘 지내고 있어?

다현 : _____

종하 : 좋아. 다 괜찮아.

다현 : _____

종하 : 그런 생각 없었는데, 왜?

다현 : _____

종하 : 그런데?

다현 : _____

종하 : 그랬구나. 글쎄, 난 아무 소리도 못 들었는데.

다현 : _____

종하 : 하지만 난 처음으로 듣는 말인 걸.

다현 : _____

종하 : 내 차는 괜찮아.

다현 : _____

종하 : 문제 없을 거야.

다현 : _____

종하 : 그러면 네 차는 어떻게 할 건데?

다현 : _____

종하 : 그래, 학교에 차 몰고 가는지 어떤지를 묻는 이유가 달리 있었구만. 공사 중에 먼지 안 쓰게 하는 게 이유는 아닌 거 같은데?

다현 : _____

종하 : 내가 차 몰고 학교 가면 태워다 드릴까?

다현 : _____

종하 : 천만에 ...

## 14. 자동차로 가?

종 하 : _____

다현 : 다 괜찮아. 고맙고. 넌 어때?

종 하 : _____

다현 : 내일 학교 차 몰고 갈 거야?

종 하 : _____

다현 : 응. 내일 아파트 근처에 공사가 있을 거거든.

종 하 : _____

다현 : 음, 주차장에 차 두지 말라는 얘기가 있었다 하더라고.

종 하 : _____

다현 : 이상하네. 여기저기서 통지가 있었다는데.

종 하 : _____

다현 : 어쨌든 큰 트럭이 왔다갔다 하면서 먼지가 많이 날 거야.

종 하 : _____

다현 : 네 차량이 손상되는 일이 있어도 괜찮다는 뜻인가?

종 하 : _____

다현 : 글쎄다. 나라면 절대로 위험은 감수하지 않을 텐데...

종 하 : _____

다현 : 어, 내 차는 지금 수리 가게에 있어.

종 하 : _____

다현 : 당근이지!

종 하 : _____

다현 : 아, 그거 참 좋은 생각이네! 고마우이!

종 하 : _____

**MY NOTES:**

## 15. Looks like rain today

Damin  : Did you see the weather forecast for today?

Dahyeon: Sorry, but I didn't see it.

Damin  : It looks like it's going to rain though.

Dahyeon: Do you think so.

Damin  : The sky is very cloudy.

Dahyeon: It's not cloudy. It's just early and the sun isn't out yet.

Damin  : It's already 9:00!

Dahyeon: Well, still that doesn't mean it will rain.

Damin  : But it might rain.

Dahyeon: But it might not rain.

Damin  : Maybe I should go back to our dorm and get my umbrella.

Dahyeon: No, uh, you don't need an umbrella.

Damin  : But it might rain.

Dahyeon: But it might not, and then you'll just waste your time going to get your umbrella.

Damin  : But if it does rain?

Dahyeon: You won't melt.

Damin  : Why are you so sure it won't rain?

Dahyeon: I'm not.

Damin  : Then why don't you want me to go get my umbrella?

Dahyeon: What are you talking about?

Damin  : It seems you don't want me to get my umbrella. Why?

Dahyeon: Well, actually I borrowed it already.

Damin  : Now I see…

Dahyeon: (hands it over) Here you go.

Damin  : Don't worry. If it rains, I'll share.

## 15. 오늘 비 올 것 같아

다민 : 오늘 일기 예보 봤어?

다현 : 아니, 안 봤는데.

다민 : 그런데 비 올 것 같은데.

다현 : 그럴 거 같다구?

다민 : 하늘에 구름이 많이 끼었어.

다현 : 구름이 낀 게 아니고, 이른 시간이라 해가 아직 안 나온 거지.

다민 : 벌써 9 시야!

다현 : 음, 그래도 비 올 거라는 생각은 안 들어.

다민 : 하지만 비가 올 수도 있지.

다현 : 하지만 비가 안 올 수도 있음.

다민 : 숙사에 돌아 가서 우산을 가지고 오는 편이 나을 듯해.

다현 : 아니, 우산은 필요 없어.

다민 : 하지만 비가 올 수도 있어.

다현 : 하지만 비가 안 올 수도 있어. 그러니까 우산 가지러 가는 시간만 낭비하는 거지.

다민 : 그래서 비가 온다면?

다현 : 빗물에 녹을 일은 없지.

다민 : 왜 비가 안 온다고 장담하지?

다현 : 장담하는 거는 아니고.

다민 : 그럼 왜 우산을 가지러 가지 못하게 하는 거야?

다현 : 무슨 말이지?

다민 : 우산 가지러 가면 안 된다는 듯이 말하고 있잖아, 왜?

다현 : 그래, 실은 내가 네 우산을 먼저 빌려 왔다는 사실.

다민 : 진짜 이유는 따로 있었구만.

다현 : (우산을 건네주며) 자, 여기.

다민 : 걱정 마. 비 오면 씌어 줄테니까.

## 15. 오늘 비 올 것 같아

다민 : 오늘 일기 예보 봤어?

다현 : _____

다민 : 그런데 비 올 것 같은데.

다현 : _____

다민 : 하늘에 구름이 많이 끼었어.

다현 : _____

다민 : 벌써 9 시야!

다현 : _____

다민 : 하지만 비가 올 수도 있지.

다현 : _____

다민 : 숙사에 돌아 가서 우산을 가지고 오는 편이 나을 듯해.

다현 : _____

다민 : 하지만 비가 올 수도 있어.

다현 : _____

다민 : 그래서 비가 온다면?

다현 : _____

다민 : 왜 비가 안 온다고 장담하지?

다현 : _____

다민 : 그럼 왜 우산을 가지러 가지 못하게 하는 거야?

다현 : _____

다민 : 우산 가지러 가면 안 된다는 듯이 말하고 있잖아, 왜?

다현 : _____

다민 : 진짜 이유는 따로 있었구만.

다현 : _____

다민 : 걱정 마. 비 오면 씌어 줄테니까.

15. 오늘 비 올 것 같아

다민 : _____

다현 : 아니, 안 봤는데.

다민 : _____

다현 : 그럴 거 같다구?

다민 : _____

다현 : 구름이 낀 게 아니고, 이른 시간이라 해가 아직 안 나온 거지.

다민 : _____

다현 : 음, 그래도 비 올 거라는 생각은 안 들어.

다민 : _____

다현 : 하지만 비가 안 올 수도 있음.

다민 : _____

다현 : 아니, 우산은 필요 없어.

다민 : _____

다현 : 하지만 비가 안 올 수도 있어. 그러니까 우산 가지러 가는 시간만 낭비하는 거지.

다민 : _____

다현 : 빗물에 녹을 일은 없지.

다민 : _____

다현 : 장담하는 거는 아니고.

다민 : _____

다현 : 무슨 말이지?

다민 : _____

다현 : 그래, 실은 내가 네 우산을 먼저 빌려 왔다는 사실.

다민 : _____

다현 : (우산을 건네주며) 자, 여기.

다민 : _____

**MY NOTES:**

## 16. The mean boss

Hyocheol : How's work these days?

Younghwa: Not so good actually.

Hyocheol : Oh, really. That's too bad. What's going on?

Younghwa: Well, it's my boss.

Hyocheol : Again? You haven't gotten along from the start.

Younghwa: That's right. He's harder on me than the others.

Hyocheol : That's not really fair.

Younghwa: I know!

Hyocheol : Did you tell him that?

Younghwa: Of course! I've said that to him several times.

Hyocheol : And still he treats you unfairly?

Younghwa: That's just the way he is. He even admitted that I was right.

Hyocheol : That's really bad. Why don't you quit?

Younghwa: I really need the money, and it's not easy to find another job.

Hyocheol : Can you talk to your boss's boss?

Younghwa: Oh no. That's not going to work.

Hyocheol : Oh? Are you sure?

Younghwa: They're married!

Hyocheol : Oh, then you really have a big problem.

Younghwa: I know. It really makes dinner time at my house tense.

Hyocheol : Why?

Younghwa: Yeah, my boss is my dad…

## 16. 심술궂은 상관

효철 : 요즘 어때?

영화 : 마음대로 잘 안 돼.

효철 : 아, 그래. 그러면 안 되는데. 뭐가 어째서?

영화 : 글쎄, 내 상사 있잖아.

효철 : 아직 그래? 처음부터 잘 안 맞았잖아.

영화 : 그래 맞아. 나만 두고 씹지.

효철 : 부당한 일이다.

영화 : 나도 그렇게 생각해!

효철 : 부당하다는 이야기는 했어?

영화 : 물론 했지! 몇 번이나 이야기했어.

효철 : 그런데도 널 여전히 부당하게 취급해?

영화 : 그 사람의 방식인 거지. 심지어는 내가 하는 말이 옳다는 거까지 인정하면서 그래.

효철 : 참 대책이 안 선다. 그만 둬 버리지 그래 ?

영화 : 살아야 하잖아. 다른 일을 찾는다는 것도 쉽지 않고.

효철 : 내가 그 상사의 상사를 만나 말해줘 ?

영화 : 아니, 아니. 그래서 해결 될 일이 아냐.

효철 : 어? 진짜 그래?

영화 : 그들은 부부인 걸!

효철 : 아하, 그럼 정말이지 큰 문제로군.

영화 : 그러게. 내 집에서 하는 식사 시간에도 긴장해야 한다니까.

효철 : 왜?

영화 : 음, 내 상사가 다름아닌 우리 아버지야.

16. 심술궂은 상관

효철 : 요즘 어때?

영화 : _____

효철 : 아, 그래. 그러면 안 되는데. 뭐가 어째서?

영화 : _____

효철 : 아직 그래? 처음부터 잘 안 맞았잖아.

영화 : _____

효철 : 부당한 일이다.

영화 : _____

효철 : 부당하다는 이야기는 했어?

영화 : _____

효철 : 그런데도 널 여전히 부당하게 취급해?

영화 : _____

효철 : 참 대책이 안 선다. 그만 둬 버리지 그래?

영화 : _____

효철 : 내가 그 상사의 상사를 만나 말해줘?

영화 : _____

효철 : 어? 진짜 그래?

영화 : _____

효철 : 아하, 그럼 정말이지 큰 문제로군.

영화 : _____

효철 : 왜?

영화 : _____

16. 심술궂은 상관

효철 : _____

영화 : 마음대로 잘 안 돼.

효철 : _____

영화 : 글쎄, 내 상사 있잖아.

효철 : _____

영화 : 그래 맞아. 나만 두고 씹지.

효철 : _____

영화 : 나도 그렇게 생각해!

효철 : _____

영화 : 물론 했지! 몇 번이나 이야기했어.

효철 : _____

영화 : 그 사람의 방식인 거지. 심지어는 내가 하는 말이 옳다는 거까지 인정하면서 그래.

효철 : _____

영화 : 살아야 하잖아. 다른 일을 찾는다는 것도 쉽지 않고.

효철 : _____

영화 : 아니, 아니. 그래서 해결 될 일이 아냐.

효철 : _____

영화 : 그들은 부부인 걸!

효철 : _____

영화 : 그러게. 내 집에서 하는 식사 시간에도 긴장해야 한다니까.

효철 : _____

영화 : 음, 내 상사가 다름아닌 우리 아버지야.

**MY NOTES:**

## About the authors:

Allen Williams was born and raised in the United States. He graduated from Murray State University with a Bachelors in Broadcast and a Masters in American Literature. He then earned a PhD while living and working in South Korea. He is the author of several textbooks for English language learning as well as for learning Korean. After spending 6 years in Korea, he moved to Japan where he lives with his wife and two sons and teaches at university.

Sulseob Jo was born and raised in South Korea. She graduated from university in South Korea with an undergraduate degree in Chinese characters. She then moved to Japan to study at Nagoya University where she earned a Masters and a PhD in Chinese literature. She is a professor teaching a wide range of subjects from Korean language to Chinese literature as well as Asian culture. She is the author of several books on learning Korean language. She and her husband live in Japan with their two sons.

www.ingramcontent.com/pod-product-compliance
Lightning Source LLC
Chambersburg PA
CBHW080853120626
46550CB00007B/2626